REINVENT YOURSELF

LEARN THE FUNDAMENTALS OF LIVING HAPPY LIFE WITH NOTHING

NARAYAN JHA

This Book is Dedicated to Supreme Power (Shri Krishna), All Teachers, My Parents, and Loved Ones.

Without the support of all, This huge task is never possible.

Inspired By Bhagwat Geeta, 3 Idiots Movie & Other Real Life Experiences

Contents

Contents

Preface

The idea behind this book came when I joined a big French MNC (Capgemini) as a fresher As the COVID-19 situation came so I use to work more than 15 hours for that company because of layoffs and other recession scenarios. I was fully destroyed internally and almost had no one who should care for all this but I learned really great lessons from that experience and many other things in my life that made me strong enough to write a whole book.

By the way, I am **Narayan Jha**, Founder of **Wakeupcoders**, A software development company that does more than build software in a very creative and unique way. This is also an achievement from my prior experiences, I have taught thousands of students about machine learning and other software development things from all around the world. Developed and worked on many software-based products and clients, Also I spent a lot of my time on hobbies like music production and created 3 Albums (Two Souls, My Illusion & My Burning Desire), Experienced the life of Merchant Navy, Not only I learned things from all these domains also made expertise on these things and created a great impact on my work areas.

Many people suggested me I should focus on only one thing cause it's really hard to learn and manage all these but personally I believe if you are capable enough to make things possible then make yourself good at all. You must use your power of intuition to make things real and your all senses (Indriya) should be focused enough in such a way that your whole body helps you to learn and adapt things in a quicker manner. This is the magic of the human body but only a few people are able to understand and utilize this power.

Finally, I decided to add a full stop and become a software engineer professionally but I really love to think beyond such things and try to spend my time to listening my inner voice of me which I usually get because of all these experiences at the age of 24. This book is precisely the result of the same.

As a lot of work-from-home opportunities are going on, I grabbed this opportunity to write a book so that my whole life experience can be shared with whosoever is required. This book's perspective is to think about simplicity. It took more than 8 months to write the whole book. I faced a lot of difficulties and challenges while writing this book because spending extra hours after your daily working hours is sometimes a tedious thing.

> *"The world's most difficult thing is just to be simple.*
>
> *- Narayan Jha"*

Thanks to all who contributed to completing this book.

Credits are available in the authors & Acknowledgement section.

Acknowledgements

It's all about the story of my school days when I did not have many friends but books were my one of super best friends, So I always had a dream of publishing my articles on books. I use to write a lot of garbage stuff at that time lol, Unfortunately, this never happened but fortunately, after a few years life taught me endlessly, amazing, and valuable lessons, This has given me enormous potential and motivation to write a whole book with good experiences.

For that, I would really love to thank Lord Krishna (My Supreme Power), My career teacher Ram Parshad (My Guru), and all the problems of my life which helped me to understand and experience all those things which I have shared in this book,

Also, it helped me to get free from most of the materialistic things in which we are trapped. While starting this book, I never imagined that it could be so a tedious process but rewarding process as well.

This has been never possible without the help of my parents (Ram Lal & Poonam Devi) and sister (Anjali Kumari) and my closest one Shailja Bizalwan. These are those people of my life who was always there for me in every struggle and successful situation of my life.

I'm gratefully thankful to Shazeb Gautam (Elder Brother) who has given his precious time and experience to help and support all aspects of my and my family's life. He is also helping a lot of people with his knowledge and experience. He is a great guy and the biggest motivation behind this book.

Other special thanks to the **Wakeupcoders Founding** members who are always there with great support for everything. This team member has Purnima Sinha (Creative Director), Simran Singh (Chief Operating Officer) Anjali Kumari (Marketing Head), and Amit Sinha (Chief Technology Officer), Every person on this team has a special and specific role with super special powers, who helped me with technology, marketing, creative content generation, and operational things as well. It could be really hard to do all this stuff alone, These are the founding members who were always there with their special powers to support.

Although after getting so much support from these great personalities, The period of my life was not so smooth, it was full of ups and downs which was something like an adventure. All these ups and downs experiences would not be worthwhile without Capgemini (My First IT Company) where I met with Tejas Mohandas (First Manager), Sameer Desai (Manager), Deepali Gaikwad (Senior Developer), Chanakya Gupta (Senior Developer), Christy Margret (Senior Developer), Jayshree Lokhande (Senior Developer), Hemalatha (Business Owner), Indira Chatterjee (Business Owner), Pradnya, Madhuri, Shobhit (Tehlka Gang Members) and many others. Learned so many things about finance and the corporate world from these amazing people.

A great Thanks to Tony Stark, A fictional character in the iron man movie that gave me enough motivation to do all these amazing things at a very small age, even this iron man exists in my real life, **Karan Jha** real iron man who is always there for me in every aspect of life. He faced a lot of problems in his life, I salute his caliber to be happy and remained strong enough to deal with these things, We both created **Day & Night, Black & White Heroes community** where we use to help people at night, Those were funny,

Exciting and Thrilled days of my life. Thanks, **Karan** for Everything.

Writing a book about your life with your experiences is an unrealistic feeling kind of process. I also got such great experiences with one of my best clients **Muskan Singh, Sukhdeep Singh, Navdeep Kaur, and many others**. It's just because of these clients I got effort and encouragement which helped me to get out of my comfort and start working on this project.

NotionPress also deserves great respect and support who enabled writers like me to share their experiences with their platform and superfast tools. By using this platform only I am able to elaborate my knowledge and let down the hectic process of writing a book

Finally, To all those people who have been part of my journey in life :

Ankur Warikoo, Akshat Shrivastava (**Youtuber &Enterpreneur**), Harish Uthayakumar (**CoFounder - BlueLearn**)

Suraj Batra, Jayant Chawla, Deepak Goswami, Shivang Jindal, Amarpreet Kaur, Sonal Khanna, Sunil Kumar, Chandan Kumar, Jayoti Parkash, Amanjot Singh (**Alpha Squad Warriors of FIS**).

Deepak Mehra, Parveen Singh, Jeewanand Semwal, and Shashank Bhardwaj (**Great Friends**)

Karan Dipak Borse (**The fire behind my all ideas**)

" In the endeavor of flying
high like eagle i forgot to chirping like a sparrow "
- Narayan Jha

Jai Shree Krishna

*"Why do you worry unnecessarily ? Whom do you fear ? Who can kill you ? The soul is neither born nor dies – **Lord Krishna**"*

I AM IRON MAN!

"*Sometimes living in ultra imaginary world will let you do outstanding things*
- Narayan Jha"

Prologue

This book "**Reinvent Yourself**" brings all those factors into consideration which makes our life difficult and bad so that we can make control of that and happy life can be made.

Eventually, if we observe for decades we generally need nothing more than five things to live a happy (Food, Shelter, Family, Pure Natural Resources, and Knowledge) and fulfilled life. The only condition for that it should be pure enough. All the sources of the book are inspired and learned from the "Bhagwat Geeta" (God Krishna) and real-life experiences.

As time has moved there are too many distractions, problems, and diseases have risen. The technology which we made for our ease purpose only That's only creating resistance for us to live a happy life. In the race of living a luxurious life and growing at a faster rate, we forgot to live a healthy life. We imbalanced our food, relationship, knowledge, and other things which are building blocks for a living good life. Just because of this, I have seen a lot of people suffering from problems, diseases, and many other things these lists are unending.

But suffering from all these is not the overall solution. We need to find out the root cause and exact reason for being suffered and we need to work on it. Only then we will be able to live with a free mind, If we will be free from the mind, We will automatically start loving things and happy life can be achieved.

There can be several reasons for failures and problems.

- Money Crisis
- Social Media Things

- Mindset
- Target Failures
- Relationships and many more

This book is not all about the technique to give you the royal cars or any good rich lifestyle but this will give you the essence of living a happy and fruitful life with whatever you have simply and informally or if you are at zero and having nothing then what are the minimalistic things required to be happy you will get to know in the chapters available in this book.

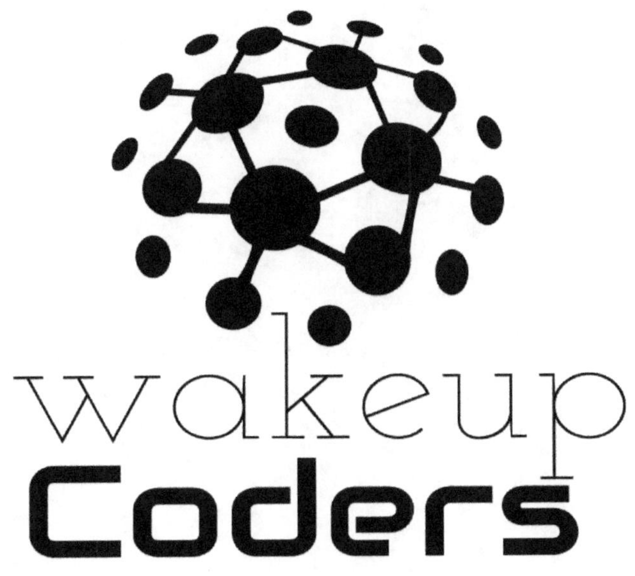

- THINK BEYOND EVERYTHING

CHAPTER ONE

Think, Money As A Tool Not As A Trap

Money is something that plays a vital role in everyone's life. It's also known by the term "MAYA" (Hindi Term). We all are surrounded by the magical power of money. For some people, it might be just a piece of paper because there might be big and multiple assets or businesses running for them But for some, its everything and they are putting huge efforts to get some of its parts so that they can get some food, cloths and other essential parts of life. But have you ever tried thinking that why there is so much difference?

Why do some people have everything, They have so many even the next generations even don't require to earn, but some have even nothing for their daily essential things. If we talk about the exact reason, It might be very tedious to find because everyone has their own situations, efforts, Thinking Standards, or techniques. Let's try to figure out the generic root cause that works for everyone's life and these differences are being created.

Think of Money As A Tool Not As A Trap

The common reason for having this difference is when the expenses are too much increased than the earnings or a person doesn't have any earnings If a person has earnings and whatever earnings he has, He doesn't know to use money as a tool, but as a trap.

"Someday, Somehow, Somewhere your investments are going to come to you by some another way.
- Narayan Jha"

For Example: If we talk about the richest people who have everything, Many of them use money as a tool, Using that money they know which assets and businesses need to be created that work for them even when they sleep. They also know the art of staying away from liabilities or unnecessary expenses, Some of them also created their liabilities into assets. In such a way, rich people have control over the time, because money is working for them and they don't have to worry about their bread and butter, In this way, good peace of mind can be achieved whereas the poor people never create assets and they stuck into the cycle of their one source of income where they need to be present all the time.

In India like countries we are also concerned about our future generations, we think to earn money so much so that the next generations should not have any problems but why so?

Do you ever have thought about what will be the economical circumstances for our future generations?

Maybe the earnings we are making today, it's going to be zero because of some kind of war or epidemic circumstances. No one knows the future. We are destroying our present just in the thought process of the future. But still considering the emotional feelings of those future generations we might consider the paper and non-paper-based assets that might help to deal with extremely bad scenarios. Also, we can consider purchasing the cheapest life insurance at the right time so that our dependents can be safe and great peace of mind can be achieved. In order to achieve those we can use a simple sequence formula. If you are at Zero then use these basic three steps.

1. Creating Incomes

Learn different skills which you are also interested to learn and even by selling them you can earn some money. Try to learn those skills which have good demand in the market so that good income streams can be made like learning about web development, blockchain, and Artificial Intelligence. These are examples of highly demanded topics in the market. Once you have generated the income you should use the second step of creating assets.

2. Planning For Assets

Using the income that you have made by selling your skills use some amount of income to invest in assets. So that those assets can work for you. Assets will work as a passive income for you. when you sleep as well these assets work as a secondary person works in place for you. Try purchasing commercial shops, business stocks, crypto, and whatever you have knowledge of. In this way, you don't have to worry about the primary income and you will be able to control your time.

3. Design your Emergency

Nobody knows about the emergency situation. create at least 2 years of expense fund handy so that in case, In any way your assets stop or you are not able to create income with your skills. These funds will work as an angel for you. you don't have to worry about anything cause you will be independent in any situation. purchase some health and life insurance that will work for you in any kind of emergency and great peace can be achieved.

If you have gained control over **PEACE OF MIND & TIME** you are a much richer person than anyone because of this power you will be able to do a lot of creative activities without worrying about anything.

Money (One form of Maya) is a kind of material energy that is being created due to our ignorance but if someone is rich with the knowledge to deal with Maya. This will hardly be going to be a trap for you.

Shree Krishna has already stated that Maya is an extension of His energy and not an illusion. The Śhwetāśhvatar Upaniṣhad also states:

māyāṁ tu prakṛitiṁ vidyānmāyinaṁ tu maheśhvaram - "Maya is the energy (prakṛiti), while God is the Energetic." Being spiritual is also one of the ways that teach you to live a happy balanced life.

Understanding balancing the money is an art otherwise it's going to be a trap for you, Have you ever seen some very rich people who are also not happy with their richness as well, Money or assets is essential but money can't buy everything, If it's not being balanced correctly then this can create diseases, relationships, and many other disorders. Having no money also sometimes becomes a problem if your family and loved ones are dependent on you. Just focus on earning money to fulfill your things, we are just focusing to earn a lot of money without any reason even if our needs and wants are fulfilled. This starts becoming a trap for us. We never tried having a full stop and made a thought, How much money is important? Most of us don't have an answer to this and we just say the more money we'll have, the more we'll be happy. That's totally wrong.

Just because we don't have an answer for this. We are on the rat race to earn infinite money and we die someday within this race itself. Sometimes we try to compromise our health for the highest-paying opportunities. This is itself a money trap when you get too much money or assets because of this greed to earn more sometimes increases.

The mindset behind this is more money means more control over things like Time, Buying Bread Butter or essential things of life till the long term so that you can be happy. Unless just having a lot of money without any reason is always bad.

Just because we are not satisfied with whatever we have we sometimes create problems for ourselves only. How to get rid of all these?

Always Remember - **Use this money as a Tool Not as a trap.**

CHAPTER TWO

Believe In Current Thinking & Instinct

We as a human all have big dreams, we want to achieve a lot of things in very less time whereas the quality of effort is directly impactful to get the achievement of dreams. The more finest and efficient efforts will be, The more probability to win a situation. whenever we want to reach a goal, There might be thousands of ways to reach that goal, but many times we never know the exact efficient path to reach there.

There are many people who are not even able to get started with their journey just because they are not able to get what track or way should be selected to achieve a goal.

JUST THINK Doing Nothing is also not a good solution. Instead of this, we can start putting our efforts into whatever resources we have, Whatever experiences we have, and Whatever Thinking and Instinct we are having. At least start with some point. This gives results that might be positive or negative. No one has come with multiple talents, and experiences from their birth. We all grow by learning from experiencing things.

Believe In Your Current Thinking & Instinct

Even no one has "**ELON MUSK**" thinking capabilities from their birth. Even he has gained experience by reading books and building products like Zip2, Paypal, and SpaceX. It all comes with experience and to get those experience we need the courage to put in our efforts. It's not only about the success part. He also got failure in building the SpaceX project, Two of his rockets were blasted with that experience he still took the third rocket into action which was successful.

Putting effort with no experience, We have to start believing in ourselves and should start believing in the current thinking process which might be definitely changed when we get some experience like Elon Musk had from the failures.

By measuring the results of returns we can start changing the thinking process and take further improved actions. Using this approach you will never be in a feeling of guilty that you had that opportunity and were not able to grab that one.

Most people in the whole world just show off that they know everything and they have their expertise on certain things but the reality is sometimes totally different, Things even change when an extremely hard situation comes. At that time current thinking and instinct only work as the most powerful tool but for that at least having faith in our thinking and confidence while executing is one of the important aspects.

Believing in your current thinking and instinct also improves the presence of the mind, It removes laziness because you never know how the situation may that person get. It's all about readiness for the next upcoming change with current knowledge and experience without getting the fear of losing something. It even doesn't apply to the whole people because if some are already happy with their current fixed routines and challenges then in those scenarios it's not compulsory but having a faith in ownself beliefs is always plus point.

Even Lord Krishna also said on believing in ourselves. He says:

> *"BELIEVE IN YOURSELF AND DO YOUR KARMA (ACTION), SUCCESS WILL FOLLOW YOU AUTOMATICALLY. DOING KARMA IS IN OUR HANDS ONLY, RESULT IS NOT IN OUR HANDS.*
> *- Lord Krishna"*

We have also seen some people believe in their thinking and they get success too with that mindset sometimes this winning might make you overconfident and this mindset also makes a person go towards failure because trying to face an unexpected situation with overconfidence also doesn't makes sense and it might demotivate that person because he might have to face a lot of problems in some cases. so it's always a great practice to be neutral and have faith in current thinking and instinct without just being overconfident so that we can be ready for all kinds of failures and winnings without being affected emotionally.

CHAPTER THREE

Bring Motivation Everyday

Motivation! Motivation!! Motivation!!! You might have heard this word from many content creators from different social network platforms. Everyone might be told the different steps and ways to be motivated toward a certain goal or thing. Motivation plays a really important role to achieve a certain goal in our life. If you are motivated you can develop skills, Have good marks in school, Perform well in Office or achieve the dream that you might have seen during your childhood days. If you are not motivated then performing any small action for achieving any kind of goal might be really tedious task.

We all want to be motivated all the time and to be motivated all the time we are contributing to the TRP (Target Rating Point) of different content creators but think is it that easy to be motivated all the time by just watching a video? It's not how things work when you don't start implementing things in your life. Implementation is the first and hard stage of bringing anything back to you.

Watching videos might definitely help you to feel high for a certain time but performing action is more important than just being motivated. There is no use in such motivation if you are not able to perform any kind of action to achieve your dream goal. If you are not having the feeling of doing action towards that thing or goal either you don't love your work or you don't really want to achieve that dream. It's always good to have clarity first on the things you really want or just to show off.

Bring Motivation Everyday

Once you decide on the goal or dream for which you get the feel of doing action and why it matters in your life then your first step is done. Sometimes we are clear about the things we want to do but by just overthinking we make our small goals look like a big piece of rock. This also discourages us to put our actions to achieve things. So once you finalized the goal don't overthink just think about a small piece of action that can be done and check the results of that effort. If that action really works then it's great. You got feedback and you are good to go for the next piece of the action. This small step's result itself is going to create an inner motivation for you to proceed ahead. This small feeling of achievement ignites the fire inside yourself to bring the further piece of the action to achieve the goal as soon as possible. This is one kind of self-motivation that also gives you the capability to self introspect as well.

Now think if that piece of action doesn't work still it's great :) because it saved a lot of your time by not going in the wrong direction. You can modify or think of a new piece of the action and check results for them which might lead to going on the right track.

"Never think big things Just start with little, It will encourage you to do big things.
- Narayan Jha "

This is one way when you don't know the track how to accomplish your dreams, you can start with yourself only without wasting much time. In many cases when we are aware of the goals also we are good at doing the action as well. The goal itself is huge that demotivates us to achieve it with our solo journey. Not everyone going to help you until or unless good results are not shown to them in return for that effort. In such cases, it's always good to break down the huge task into smaller tasks. when the tasks are broken down we can create a timeline for achieving the smaller goals. For example, we can create timelines in a small manner like creating a one-month or week plan in which the group of those smaller goals needs to be achieved. while creating a plan for such things it's always good practice to consider the priority, risks, complexity, and cost around that action. You might also get a lot of failures and unknowns during completing the tasks. To understand the behavior of unknowns you can count one more task which can be named **"ENABLER"** which will give you enough time to understand the unknowns and complete the task without having much pressure.

This will give you motivation after completing the small tasks successfully, also it works as an independent entity that never blocks other things, and in this way, teamwork can also be performed which can speed up things as well. While performing such kind of plan you always need an experience in proactive planning which also comes with practice. when all the small tasks are completed we can merge together to see the huge bigger picture.

We can take inspiration from "**Manjhi**" (The Mountain Man of India) Manjhi carved a path between Wazirgang and Atri through a 360 ft long, 30 ft wide, and 25 ft high hillock. He achieved the milestone after working for 22 years, from 1960 to 1982. Manjhi's effort reduced Atri to Wazirgang distance to 15 km from 55 km, giving relief to Gehlorians. Behind all this, he had a really sad story but he achieved all this thing alone.

To conclude, everything resides in ourselves, Make yourself active enough with a creative mindset to understand your goals, and start with your first plan of achieving things. Try to figure out the risks, failures, backup plans to achieve your dreams and start achieving your things in baby steps so that you only can be your motivation source by just putting in small efforts.

CHAPTER FOUR

Risk – The Finest Teacher Of Your Life

RISK - A smallest 4-character word that sounds too horrible. It's not only horrible for poor or middle-class people. It also implies for every rich class people as well. If we talk about its definition then we can say that any uncertain scenario that we never want to happen works opposite to our planning or action. Risk is something that works exactly the same for everyone without any kind of discrimination.

If we see rich people like Ambani, Adani, and Elon Musk. They also go through risk even though, their chances of risk are much higher than any of the common man. The risk might be anything it might be related to Health, Financial, Business, Research, and many others what exactly is the thing these people are capable of taking higher risks and also higher returns but on the other hand common man is just stuck under the common things itself.

There are a lot of people who come under the common category and they can't even afford to take 0.001 % of the risk also sometimes some people are not even able to think to grow just they don't take any kind of risk.

Manage Your Risk

Remember !! If you really want to grow and get something there might definitely some risk would be there. Doing nothing just because there is a risk is sometimes much more expensive than just sitting idle and playing safe.

What exactly is the difference between these two categories of people? Why do rich people become rich and able to do all the stuff that he/she wants to do whereas other people is too much busy with their routine and systems that they are not able to think beyond that?

Risk can be one of the greatest teachers if you can start facing instead of just ignoring or getting scared of it. A lot of people just want to ignore just because they don't have the courage to face the risk that's one of the reasons they are not able to get the things they want. There are a lot of other things as well for which we might not consider taking risks like health, family, friends, etc. This chapter will only be considering taking risks that can be originated like businesses, skills, finances, or whatever the childhood dream. If you read the first chapter of the book "Think Money As A Tool, Not As A Trap". Rich people have a lot of assets and businesses that work for them and they are able to buy the time and peace of mind because of passive streams without worrying about bread & butter. It also not implies to those who are stuck in the cycle of greediness but if you have enough time and resources then you will be to think much deeper about the risks without ignoring things and having a fear of losing things with whatever the current thinking and instinct you are having.

Rich people makes risks as their best friends. They are very much clear about their friends We can't say that rich people never fail but the motivation of standing up and fighting again comes with a calculation. Not with a hit and trial. Otherwise, you might also end up losing every time, and also you might lose the motivation and energy for doing anything. They create a lot of metrics to know the risks very clearly so that they can take the next piece of action wisely. In other simple words, they love taking risks and having higher returns just because they have the art of managing the risks, calculating, and wisely mitigating them. By monitoring all the metrics of risks rich people are able to save a lot of energy and effort which can be utilized for taking further actions or maybe for enjoyment by doing a world tour. Let's try to figure out a few of the common things that we can also consider while taking any kind of risk and that will help us as well as part of metrics and we will be able to take risks without losing the energy and motivation.

Rich people thinks the below mentioned thinks before actually taking any kind of risk, Just because these steps helps get enough probability

1. Calculates the risk (How much is the risk, Is It too high or can be accomodated)

2. Check the appetite

3. Probability of risk

4. Impact of Risk

5. Alternatives (If have)

5. Backup Plan for that risk

6. Prioritizing the risks if multiple

7. If fails then consider it as the learning and plan for next action.

As like rich people You should start taking risk and start your learning with it, atleast with 1% or 2% of your things for which which you can't be worried, because it will help you to develop the art to deal with risks or unexpected situations. You should be good enough with knowledge for such things while taking risks so that you must know the results behind it and learn from it. Sometimes such learning has capability to give you best possible returns because not everyone in this whole world is trying to deal with risk and learn from it but those few who accepts risks and learns from it. They develop the capability to deal with fear of losing something and achieve the amazing stages of their life. once you learnt the way to work with risks. You will start playing with it and you can also be one of the game changers of your life.

CHAPTER FIVE

Art Of Writing Your Own Future

In our human life, Most of us we all are surrounded by the feelings of the past and future. This can be good, bad, or mixed depending upon our actions or experiences we had in our past or about the future as well. If we talk about the future we sometimes stuck thinking about the results that we want to have but currently, we are not having. This kind of thinking also ruins our present. If we just keep thinking about our future because that result needs sufficient efforts in the present so that we can get the expected results in the future. I am not saying You should never think about your future but ending up stuck in that thinking cycle is not good, Instead of that spend some time planning the future with calmness and the rest of the other time spent on its execution. This is because we only have control over the execution and we should spend a maximum of time with our 100% execution effort. The execution efforts give you real feedback which you might not be able to get while planning or thinking about the future phases. That's why this approach saves a lot of time and energy. The results of your action can bring some good motivation as well.

Writing your growing future

On the other hand this sometimes never applies to those who are having really great support from luck. You might be laughing by reading this term because on one side I am talking about the real execution facts and on the other hand, I am adding luck but it's really true. Your luck also plays a great role in getting something back to you. You might have seen people who do really less amount of effort but they get more than they expected. Such results are the magic of our past actions that work on that scenario unwillingly or unknowingly. Just because we are not able to correlate that current action with that result, Most people would definitely call this thing a stroke of luck. You never get anything free whatever you generally do you get results which you might get early or might get with delay too but you will definitely get someday so we can say that even luck doesn't work without effort.

The fixed thing that is in our hands is living in the present and taking planning and efforts wisely so that a good future can be created and a good past too. Instead of just thinking about future or past, believe in your current thinking and instinct and take action. A lot of people go to astrologers and palmists to know their future and modify it with some remedy. We can't say astrology is bad and it doesn't work, It's also one of the greatest sciences but you must be aware that your efforts are the biggest tool that can change any kind of science as well. Just because we are lazy and don't have the courage to plan things, bear the failures and take actions we need a remedy.

Those who know the art of writing their own future create histories. It's not that easy but such people change things in such a way that they want. Instead of messing with the things in your brain Just write your past experience results somewhere which will definitely work as a guide for you and whatever things you might planning or thinking about your future write it down somewhere. Don't let these things become a burden for you. once you have written your prior experience about the past and future that you want to achieve. Live in present and think in 6 steps way which will help you to either get your goals with your actions or exit at right time without wasting time and energy.

1. Clarity about the goals

The first step is always to get clarity about your goals or dreams for which you are planning to perform certain actions. You might use your notes of past experience if something related you might get so that the same mistakes can be avoided. There is nothing to worry about if there is no such experience too but having clarity about that goal is very much important. Think about the 360 degrees of that thing whether you really want that thing or not. It's always good to leave it in the early stage itself if that thing doesn't help you in your life or you extremely don't require that thing.

2. Risks

Now you are very much clear about the goals of things you want. If it's unnecessary just leave it in the early stage otherwise take the next step and check all the risks associated with it. You might again take help from your past experiences if you have such. You can check the chapter **"RISK - *The finest teacher of your life"*.** This will help you check the risk-related things about that goals.

3. Exit or Leave Plan

Having clarity about the seriousness of your goals and risks always gives you the best probability of getting that goal otherwise never waste your energy, money, or time on that thing. We only have efforts in our hands still there is also some probability of being failed in achieving that goal. There are many uncertain conditions that might also be there. You must also be ready for that If you are ready for such scenarios too. At the time of failure, you still have the motivation and energy to stand up again and fight with a different style because you were already prepared for these kinds of days. Always creating an exit plan or when-to-leave plan, Instead of just holding a bad thing for long with no good results is also not a great idea.

4. Planning the actions towards that results

Create small steps to achieve that goal, Perform with 100% energy to achieve that thing. All of your senses should be focused enough so that there should not be any risk or failure. When your body starts supporting you to achieve a thing you actually start getting things at a faster rate. Never overburden your body or mind with extra effort. We should always focus on performing long-term efforts. because the long-term impact of efforts can bring you legendary things.

5. Being consistent with efforts

Being consistent is an art, In the journey of achieving your dreams even if you are getting good results performing the same thing, again and again, becomes sometimes boring. Being bored is also part of human nature. Instead of leaving the thing permanently take breaks at regular intervals but always be consistent with your efforts.

6. Constantly Monitoring the Results

It might drag you to perform any kind of action in the present and you might end up being stuck in that cycle Also if you are not able to get the expected goals or results this can also be the reason for disappointment and become a bad past. If the feelings are very good we also sometimes never let perform any good action because we are generally stuck in the feeling of enjoying the good times that might we get in the future or we had in past. Now think regarding the past time it's really hard to change but this will really help you get feedback and learn from it so that you can change with the actions.

These six steps can help anyone to start writing the future journey. while performing all these steps there is going to have a lot of ups and downs which will teach you real-life lessons. Instead of getting disappointed by the lessons of life just make a note of it, learn from it and move on. This attitude is gonna change your whole world and you will start writing your future in your own way.

CHAPTER SIX

Understanding Reason For Being

In this whole universe everything which takes birth, Death for that thing is always fixed. We all have a fixed duration to live. Some people live more than 100 years and some have limited time. No one has the access to control the birth and death of any individual. We all need to do our respective work while living for that duration. we are all aware of this thing but still, most of us always ignore this. There are some people who understand this thing very well and such people use each second of life span very efficiently.

Some people are very much clear about their reasons for living and they take necessary actions at the right time. They are able to achieve everything that may have desired. Just because they know the reasons for being at a right time. Understanding your living perspective gives you much more clarity to plan your things in a deeper way. You can understand the risks in a good manner. These pieces of information can help you to create much safer and better decisions that have more probability to achieve your things.

There are also some categories of people who don't even bother about finding the reason for being. They even never know what they want to be in your life. They don't know what will be their earning sources which is going to help them in uncertain conditions.

Helping Others is the Real Purpose of Life

Such people sometimes face a lot of bad times in their upcoming future. They also have a bunch of excuses to talk about their failures. That's not a good thing. If you are not able to do or achieve anything, You are only the reason for the same. Just ask yourself a question, Why you haven't tried to find the ways through that you can achieve your things? Even that question becomes sometimes more worst when you even don't know what you want to be or achieve.

There is nothing bad if you are not aware of the things you want and even if it's not compulsory to have those but any kind of situation blaming others and finding excuses is very bad. At least you should be aware enough to deal with your bad situation and help yourself without becoming a burden to others.

Just try new things, Do some effort on any side with a hit-and-trial method and see what suits you the most, Try to find out the things that you love the most, You enjoy doing those kinds of stuff. Those efforts should help you and on the other side if you are able to find something that also has good impacts on nature on others. You have achieved the real purpose of your life.

If you still don't get what is the real purpose of your life and reason for being. You started feeling disturbed with feelings of loneliness because not all people are roaming without purpose. Others might be busy with their respective things. Then you can just start helping others, It gives the real inner peace. Helping others should be the real purpose of everyone's life. In bhagwat Geeta it's also written as.

"datavyam iti yad danam
diyate 'nupakarine
dese kale ca patre ca
tad danam sattvikam smrtam"

This means - *"Charity given out of duty, without expectation of return, at the proper time and place, and to a worthy person is considered to be in the mode of goodness".*

"yat tu pratyupakarartham
phalam uddisya va punah
diyate ca pariklistam
tad danam rajasam smrtam"

This means - *"But charity performed with the expectation of some return, or with a desire for fruitive results, or in a grudging mood, is said to be charity in the mode of passion."*

We should start with charity work without the expectation. This gives us the real chance to feel free from ourselves and found the real god which is our inside only. When you start helping others this might also become a chance that might gives you the another vision to see the whole world.

This vision is not gonna help you to Re-Invent Yourself but also change the whole world with your small peice of actions only.

"Be like a flower that never forgets to spread the fragrance until it dies.
- Narayan Jha"

Time is Super Power

Time is another name for supreme power. Its also been said that time is another form of energy. It all depends on you how you want to utilize this energy. You might have seen that the efforts done at right time always give you the best results. There is no use for such efforts which are not done at the right time that's why time is another superpower. A lot of people don't know the ways to manage this power and this becomes the reason for their lifetime pain.

We all wish for different things in different stages of our life. A student wishes to become Doctor, Engineer, Scientist, Policeman, and other. A businessman wishes to increase his business in different countries. An old age person might want to spend the maximum of their time with their loved ones just because they are in the last stage of their life. It's all about the game of time and things change with time. We can also say that time is another biggest tool that converts happiness to sadness or vice versa. You might not have all days of life happy and not all days as sad too. This is life. These create the ups and downs cycles of life.

Now the question is what is the right way to utilize this energy in an efficient way because if you are able to manage your time in a good way then you will be energetic all the time. You can do all those efforts that you want to do to get your favorite thing in your life. We can use a model called the Urgent VS Important model which will help us to prioritize our work in such a way that we can achieve anything without impacting our important things.

<table>
<tr><td></td><td>URGENT</td><td>NOT URGENT</td></tr>
<tr><td>IMPORTANT</td><td><u>Quadrant I</u>
urgent and important
DO</td><td><u>Quadrant II</u>
not urgent but important
PLAN</td></tr>
<tr><td>NOT IMPORTANT</td><td><u>Quadrant III</u>
urgent but not important
DELEGATE</td><td><u>Quadrant IV</u>
not urgent and not important
ELIMINATE</td></tr>
</table>

Important VS Urgent

This important and urgent matrix looks like the above chart and contains four different sections. Using these four sections of this basket you will be easily able to categorize your work with its priorities.

1. Urgent & Important

If you have a lot of tasks to complete. Think about the urgent and important tasks first. These are those things that can never be declined in any case. You must be clear with the results and efforts for the same. Put those tasks into the Urgent & Important basket. Add those to your timeline so that your attention can be achieved.

2. Not Urgent But Important

Now think about those tasks which are not urgent to do but important. For example, having food and doing exercise are not urgent but its really important. You never need to fix the strict deadlines for the same and things can be scheduled later. Make sure you are focusing on such things, Sometimes those tasks which are urgent and not important we generally ignore and face a lot of problems in the future. Once you ignore having good food and doing exercise your life is gonna face really hard times in the future. In the future when health issues will come you will never able to go into the past and change the time so it's always better to stay awake at the right time so that a good future can be made, a good past as well.

3. Urgent But Not Important

There is another category which is known as *"Urgent But Not Important"*. In this things needs to do done urgently but that's not much important. This is the case where you can not schedule further because it urgently needs to be done. We can use such tasks to delegate to other people. In this way, we can utilize our time in an efficient way and save a lot of time which can be used further to complete the category one and category two tasks.

4. Not Urgent And Not Important

It's always good practice to leave those tasks which are not urgent and not important. Never focus on such things which are not even urgent and not even important. You can add such tasks in some queues. Maybe that will be required in future scenarios and can be added to the first three categories when it will be required on another upcoming day.

Everyone lives in different stages of their life. You might be children, an Adult, or Old. This formula is going to be really helpful to make the best use of your time.

Lord Krishna also said something great about the time. He says :

"*"Among all kind of killers, time is the ultimate because time kills everything."*
– Lord Krishna"

Even Krishna says time is one of the greatest killers. Just be aware of your time. Plan your things efforts and risks on a timely basis so that you can achieve everything in your life in a timely way.

CHAPTER EIGHT

Get Help From Supreme Powers

In this whole universe, we all are surrounded by supreme power. It's a kind of energy that works as a cover for all types of flora and fauna. Some people believe in this power some don't. Still, without any kind of discrimination, this energy or power always supports to everyone. This is a mercy of supreme power. You might have seen different kinds of natural resources like Air, Fire, Clouds, Water, and many others which possess some kind of energy in itself that helps every flora and fauna to survive on planet earth.

Not sure about the people who don't believe in the existence of God or supreme powers, Do they know how our heart pumps without our any actions, or do we have control over the breadth which we take automatically without any effort? How this air flows and why water floats? Why all these are created helps us to survive. We have no answers for all these. We even don't know what happened when a human dies still we live with ego taking all the credit for things and we say "I have Done it!!".

Get Help From Supreme Powers

Reality is there is something super powerful exists which takes care of all these things without taking credit but we humans just by discovering a few concepts start playing with these powers. Sometimes we try to control these energies for the sake of our benefit. No one wants to understand the consequences behind these. That's the reason epidemic-like scenarios occur and nature resets itself with just one click.

There is no use for such temporary pleasures that we seek by taking advantage of nature with long-term pain. Our sciences for which we are proud and we take credit for the theories itself sometimes contradict themselves. We can't fully trust the science that we are using. The science behind the supreme powers is endless and undiscoverable. You can't create any kind of instrument or machine through that you can find answers to all these until or unless these supreme powers don't want.

It's still just an approximate number that there are 200 billion galaxies discovered by scientists. You can imagine the number of stars and planets which might exist in these galaxies. It's that huge even we can't think. We can imagine the supremeness of the creator of all these universes and lives. How smartly all things are being managed and systematically working together without disturbing each other. We can call it the god's smartest automation system that humans are just replicating and feeling happy. The reality is we can't create anything like supreme powers have created.

There are a few tools that help us to get connected with the supreme powers. Meditation and Chating work really great to establish the connection between the supreme powers. Meditation has several benefits as well, It gives you good mental health, and when we do chanting it actually produces good vibrations which work as a positive power that encourage us to get connects ourselves with the supreme power. In every country, there are different ways of doing meditation and chatting, Try to find out your favorite way over the internet that works much better for you to get yourself connected with the supreme power.

For me, lord Krishna is a supreme power who has told us the real path to live a happy life. He explained all the perspectives of our problems and their solutions through different holy books, The repository of such holy books has enormous potential to think beyond materialistic things and build a capability to know the supreme powers even for the programming kind of stuff used to exists in our ancient times as well. Ayurveda is the Veda which provides all such information and NASA scientist also found that Sanskrit is one of the best languages for A. I which is our futuristic technology.

"Whenever dharma declines and the purpose of life is forgotten, I manifest myself on earth. I am born in every age to protect the good, to destroy evil, and to reestablish dharma." – Lord Krishna

Even receiving so many things from the supreme powers not having gratitude for all those things is also not good. We should be thankful to God for everything we have. We are having a beautiful life, food, air, water, family, friends, and whatnot. Whatever you are receiving whether it is good or bad. Just be thankful for everything.

As these superpowers have so much potential you can ask for everything whenever you are in a bad feeling or whatever you want in your life just believe in them once and ask for help from supreme powers because when the logic of humans ends from there the magic of god starts. We are stuck in the greed of materialistic things just because we think that those things are limited, For nature all those things that human desires it's just the smallest thing for these powers and they have endless sources. The only thing is just to be patient, do your actions honestly and believe in that magic of supreme power you will never know when and how yours things will be accomplished.

"Its True, There is no god in stones, But Yes these stones helps you to remind that god is everywhere.
- Narayan Jha"

CHAPTER NINE

Our Solo Journey Of Life

Mindset is everything, We all must believe in this quotation because think if you are born into a very rich family then you are gonna have a really rich mindset which you might learn from the environment of businesses, in that case, earning a lot of money is going to be the easiest task for you. You can have a good mindset about your health system as well, you are gonna have really good health as well. Whatever the kind of mindset you have, You are gonna become like that. It's all about mindset. Those people who own a strong mindset, They know the reality behind these materialistic things and such people live a very happy life with whatever they are having. Only a strong mindset gives you the ability to fly above the clouds of problems and not much worrying about materialistic things otherwise there is no one who has taken anything from this world when died.

We all are stuck in this whole world just because of our wrong mindset even the biggest investor **"Rakesh Jhunjhunwala"** of the Indian stock market took nothing from this whole world when he died and said at last - **"My worst investment has been my health. I would encourage**

everybody to invest the most in that". Again the game was of mindset. Similarly, we should always be aware of the mindset behind our alone journey of life, We came into this world alone with nothing and have to go alone as well with nothing. This doesn't mean you should leave your parents or loved ones alone and live a lonely life.

Solo Journey of Life

It's about understanding your journey of life that eventually you alone have to decide in which direction you have to go. There are many families who even don't allow their children to think, only parents take all their decisions. In such a way, children will never be able to develop the capability to take important decisions independently in their life and always live with dependency.

Those people who understand the mindset behind the solo journey of life. They live their life in their own way. Such people never live their life with any kind of FOMO (Fear Of Missing Out) or anything. Life is something that gives you everything at every point. You might get good and bad experiences from that you are gonna learn a lot of things. As per your learning capability life also gives you a lot of gifts as well whatever that you deserve as per your efforts on learnings or experiences. It's similar to solo travelling by bus from one state to another in a country or you might take the feel of travelling from one country to another In the end you are just doing this journey alone. While travelling you might get a taste of different foods, cultures, technologies, businesses or any other thing that you can consider. Life gives you things in its own way. The amazing thing about this journey is that you can't simply run away otherwise life might give you some worst lessons as well.

> *"If nobody cares about your love Try to connect your imagination with feelings. Even a non living thing will start loving you - **Narayan Jha**"*

In the journey of life when you live with your solo journey mindset. You learn a lot of lessons for likewise.

Patience:

Life might give you a chance to judge your patience with whatever favourite thing you are trying to achieve with your alone's effort. You might not be going to learn this if you already have a millionaire background and everything automatically works for you. For such an experience you only have to act on it only then this life will help you to be patient.

Prioritizing:

When you live the journey of solo life this will also teach you how to prioritise your things. This is one of the amazing Art because if you are not able to prioritise your important things then you are gonna have nothing and end up losing every game of life.

Confidence:

when you will start having patience and started prioritizing your things you might definitely be going to fight with the problems. Not sure you all are going to solve but even a single thing you are able to solve in your life. It will give you another one to solve as well. In this way, you will start feeling confident and start taking independent actions or decisions. The more problems you will solve you will understand life and the more confidence you are gonna have.

Dematerialized Mindset:

when you start putting a lot of effort into something you actually start getting the value for that thing because to achieve something you have to put in a lot of your effort, solve problems, find a track and a lot more things needs to be done. After doing a lot of effort you actually start getting your mindset of dematerialization. You then actually know the real importance of materialistic things. You only give importance to those things which really add value to you not other than that.

Understanding Tolerance Ability:

Life teaches you to understand the tolerance ability by having a lot of failure according to your struggle or risk appetite. You become tolerant when you face problems and feel satisfied with the thing in your life but for developing such skills you are at least required to put some action. In this way, you start exploring yourself also.

Independence:

A solo living mindset comes with greater responsibility for yourself, Everything depends on you But at the same time your independence gives you greater flexibility, You can use any approach, any idea or anything that you wish to solve your problems. There is no such restriction or any single way to solve a particular problem. You are the master of your time, you do with it whatever you want. you don't require anything other than yourself for your own happiness.

Responsible:

Managing all your things with your independence gives you a sense of responsibility. This feeling makes your self capable enough to live an independent life. Once you are independent and you are not attached to anything, You will start living a happy life cause the remote of your happiness you only hold on your hand. Whatever or whenever you want to do with your life, You will be able to do that.

Dreams:

Now what you dream of or what you desire for yourself is not encashed in the norms of our conventional daily life. You are more open-minded, more willing to take risks and more addicted towards the adventure of exploring the unknowns of your life. This helps you to accept real and new challenges and solve them without hesitating and gives you the ability to achieve the dreams that you might have seen in your childhood days or any stage of your life.

Love & Compassion:

This could be one of the most important things when you get to learn travel about yourself when travelling solo in your life. You travel for yourself, to re-discover yourself, to experiment with your life, to explore what's in you. whether conscious or not, a solo mindset serves as a catalyst for the love for oneself, This gives you the constant ease of introspection.

As someone said, if you learnt to love yourself, you'll learn to love and have compassion for your surroundings, friends and even every stranger. It also depends on how open and receptive you are while communicating your life and how you decide to interact with your changing environment.

Life teaches us all these factors in a direct or indirect way, Life might give you many more chapters to cover depending upon your capability just learn those with a happy smile. Only those will be able to pass the exam of life who attends all the lectures of life. We can say that our life is also one of the greatest masters that teaches us through real experiences. It all depends on you whether you want to learn or not. Those who never stop learning and who never stop travelling the solo journey of life. They become the game changers in their and other life as well. The choice is yours what you want to be :).

CHAPTER TEN

Bring Failure To Motivation

Failures are part of life Not only for humans but for all the animals who are living on this planet. All get fail in some sort of doing or achieving things in their ways. It doesn't mean we should be disappointed or we should quit. It's all about the vision or way of looking at the situation, In one way we can quit everything after being failed because of disappointment, or in another way, We can bring failure as motivation, In this way, we can count a failure as an exploration of new ways from which you never get success.

We all should consider failure as a tool that encourages us to bring success in our life if it's being understood in the right way. There are very few people who know to work with such a tool. You have to practice to learn from the failures, It's a continuous learning process. Whole life we can get to learn things from our failures. Failure makes a person realize the importance of that success or thing that a person might be trying to achieve in their life.

Bring Failure To Motivation

"Bad Time is always necessary, Cause you never can feel the glory of the spotlight without darkness.
- Narayan Jha"

Generally, it's a human tendency when someone gets things very easily, Many times people don't bother about those, but something if someone has achieved with huge hard work and failures for that thing a person always takes care. It makes you realize the real value of that achievement. Also, the feel of enjoyment is going to be different when you get success after being failed many times.

Basically, it's just a mind game there is nothing like failure or success exists, It's just made by man to measure progress, and many times we end up comparing others' successes with our failures and it becomes the reason for stress in our life. Just think, if someone wants to buy a car, He purchased it as well it becomes a success for him on the other hand there is someone who never bothers to buy that same car he already succeeded in the purchase of his mind. so always understand your hunger value and if you are able to live satisfied with that you already won that game, it's just about the mindset, All people have a different definition of success and failure in their life. We got this amazing life this is even great success.

Focus on understanding your appetite, Create your definition of successes and failures, and Learn from the failures only that is going to guide you on the right track towards achieving your success. The only condition is you should be learning from the failures with a great smile.

CHAPTER ELEVEN

Experiencing & Exploration

Experience and Exploration an influential art that plays a significant role in someone's life. We as a human do a lot of things to fulfill the needs of our life. For that, we have to perform certain efforts so that in return we get things as per our requirements. For Instance, if someone is hungry then he has to perform certain things like grabbing the food from the kitchen, the Nearest store, or a restaurant so that after eating that food a person can be satisfied.

This also requires some amount of effort. Similarly, we do perform different actions to satisfy our other requirements. This is the basic need of every living organism but a Human is a special animal that has wants even after getting good food, cloth, shelter, and basic needs. He wants to live a luxurious life as well with expensive phones, cars, and many other materialistic things. For most of us, we are already fulfilled with our daily needs or may not be with wants, For those who haven't anything, Such people also get their needs fulfilled in some other ways. Now why I am talking in this about our needs and wants? Just because of these only, we do a lot of actions by running behind our needs and wants which need to be experienced and explored. By just running behind our needs, wants, or goals we sometimes just start running unnecessarily behind all such things but this is somehow wrong. We need to explore things and experience their results.

Experiencing & Exploration

It's like not doing anything without any understanding once you start doing things with exploration and experience way we generally start finding the efficient way to fulfill your requirements. We start questioning things with "**WHY**" & "**HOW**".

Our life is not about reaching the end. It's about enjoying the journey that we travel every day. but nowadays we don't have time for experiencing and exploring each moment of life. We all just build habits to get our things done quickly because of this we are suffering the journey of our life and we are not enjoying it. To start experiencing and exploring your life you have to start doing those things which you really love.

Not everyone might get a chance to do those things which they love but this never comes with an option it's about choice, you have to find out excuses to get some time from other important things so that you can do those which you love then only you will start experiencing and exploring your life. For those who are stuck in everyday's hectic schedule, They can just get 10% of the time for those things which help their soul to nourish and slowly increase with some amount by time.

If you don't know what you really love, still no worry, You can start with some random stuff like travelling you are going to explore and experience different things from other states or country. You start learning some skills may be like guitar or any instrument which will help you to experience and explore yourself. Basically exploration and experience are both cousins. when you are not aware about anything with exploration you starting learning about those things when you get adapted with things its result becomes experience of your life.

Always have the courage to experience and explore your life which will give you the real purpose to live because needs are also being fulfilled by the other animals, There is no difference if we are also in the same track. If you are born with a human body its bone to you and you should take advantage of this. Once you start living a purpose driven life with experiencing and exploration way, Congratulations you have cracked the **code** of living happy life and you have reinvented youself.

CHAPTER TWELVE

The Art Of Saying "NO"

There are different kinds of people in this whole world, Everyone lives in a different style, and All have different ways of thinking, working, and understanding things. In simple words you try to categorize people in some way, we can categorize with **Introverts & Extroverts.** I have categorized these two section because the title of this chapter is all about this only. You can create any category of people there is no such hard and fast rule. Extroverts seem to those people who know the art of telling their feelings or things to others, They might be very good communicators, On the other hand, Introverts are those who are a little hesitant to tell their feelings to others. It doesn't they are not good at communication but such people sometimes think a lot while telling something, They try to make other people happy first because such people care about the feelings of others and generally such people love their self-company most. Honestly Speaking: I am an Introvert :). The biggest problem with introverts, there is no such word as "**NO**" in their dictionary. Saying "NO" is very much difficult for such people because they don't want to upset anyone. Such people worry about what others will think of them or how the other person is going to react. Maybe they might lose favor, Such kind of thoughts generally floats on such people.

If you are one of them or like me, This chapter is especially for you. In this section, we will learn some cool things about the art of saying "**NO**".

The Art Of Saying "NO"

Cause NO MEANS NO - By the way, this is not PINK Movie Dialogue, Jokes Apart.

Sometimes we just don't want to say "NO" because we are afraid of how the other person is going to behave. It sounds very scary that the person won't like you anymore or be upset with you. However, it's always good to say "No", This can be sometimes the kindest and best thing.

You should think in such a way - If the person is really your good friend, He'll understand In other words, if it's meant to be, it will be. You should also make sure that your time is also important, Learn to protect it and save it for the things that you really want to do in your life. Everyone is having limited time in their life and time waits for no one. When you say "no" to something that you don't really want to do, you are giving yourself the freedom to spend your time doing something you really love, or maybe to be available for new opportunities!

It's ok to say "no," especially if you learn how to say it in a clear and kind way. People will respect you even more when you can give them a straightforward answer. Let's learn some of the common ways to say no in a respectful and polite way.

"NO" for any kind of invitation

- I appreciate the offer, but I can't.
- I'm honored, but can't.
- I'd love to, but I can't.
- I appreciate the invitation, but I am completely booked.

"NO" when you are not having time

- I appreciate the offer, but I can't.
- I'm honored, but can't.

- I'd love to, but I can't.
- I appreciate the invitation, but I am completely booked.

"NO" when you are not interested

- It doesn't sound like the right fit.
- I'm not sure I'm the best for it.
- I believe I wouldn't fit the bill, sorry.
- It's not a good idea for me.

"NO" for any reason at all

- It doesn't sound like the right fit.
- I'm not sure I'm the best for it.
- I believe I wouldn't fit the bill, sorry.
- It's not a good idea for me.

"NO" casually - less polite

- Mm-Mm
- I'm all set.
- I'm good.
- Not right now.

Things come with practice. Start saying "No" in your own way or take the above ways for practice. Hope it's gonna help you and you are gonna able to save a lot of time for yourself and your loved ones.

CHAPTER THIRTEEN

Believe In System

The system can bring you the legendary stuff, it's just a system that makes big things capable enough to run in an automated way. If you talk about me, From my school days I use to learn programming skills, Also I use to work with software engineers and different startups. Generally, in a small-scale organization, there is no such automated and huge system that works because in a startup there are several things a founder might have to consider. In small organizations tiny and manual system generally works because the mass of startups is very small as compared to the big organizations.

Can you fire the bullet without the system of a pistol, I think **NO**, The speed of a bullet is going to be tremendous when it joins a system. Similarly, the growth of an organization or someone's life can go to the next level if it gets connected and worked with any kind of system. This whole universe is also a kind of system designed by god which works together and perform their respective tasks.

I joined my first MNC (Multi National Company) Capgemini through college placement, I was trained as a software developer role but as a fresher, I got a chance to work as Business Analyst who is responsible to analyse the whole business and helps the business owner to take the proactive decisions.

Believe In System

I was worried at that time working as a business analyst because it was impacting my resume after few months i got chance to work as a software engineer. but in later stage of my life when i connected the dots i found myself lucky that i got a chance to learn the system of that huge organisation.

"*Believe in system, work with it then see System will change things for you.*
    - Narayan Jha"

Many people suggested me to join a startup because in small organisation most of the task is going to be done by single person so learning curve is really great but in big tech giants i was able to learn about the huge automated design that works with its own with different components interacting each other. My skills were already sharped about software development cause from school days i was practicing and working with professionals

In Capgemini, It was like a huge team player whereas the input of one person becomes the output of other with very less amount of effort a huge company is able to run with a automated and efficient way just because of its architecture designed in a really great way. Basically a system is something that has different dedicated components which functions together in such a way to complete the one vision. A ideal system has really good quality of components you can consider compoenehts as a employees if we talk about a big organisation way. Those components must be ready to work with fixed steps for fixed scenarios.

Once the steps are fixed and components are trained for it, The timing and synchronization between them play really crucial role to complete a specific task. once all those components work together it's works like a big factory just because of this huge legendary things can be accomplished with a good system. We also must know the art of designing the system of our life as well, whatever the dreams we have like finance, health, knowledge just try to figure out in which those ways you can create the design of your life, While designing the system of life make sure you have the skills like patience perseverance and dedication which is a building block of creating any best design. There will be many failures, risks as well. Just be in yourself and create own system of life.

You will be able get everything with this system, Once you start having faith in your own system and this system starts working for you, This can bring you the life long happiness to you and your loved ones.

CHAPTER FOURTEEN

The Era Of Social Network

In earlier days we used to have a lot of time for doing things that matters to us. Nowadays we don't have enough time to spend with ourselves because we have social media. Social media is not a bad thing, In earlier days we had limited usage of social media because we never use to have smartphones, unlimited data, and other resources through that we can connect with social media.

The Era Of Social Network

After a few years of efforts by big tech giants (Reliance, Airtel, etc) played a great smart game. These tech giants have given an enormous amount of data for usage. This data played the role of a new type of drug that made people addicted to it. This connectivity of the internet has welcomed many new participants in social media like Tik Tok, Instagram, WhatsApp, Facebook, Twitter, and many others.

All these networks have a great bad impact on the people which can be followed as.

1. Precious Time

These Apps killed our precious time, which can be utilized for doing great stuff like learning skills, Spending time with family and friends, or discovering something new.

2. Impact on Health

In our childhood, we use to have a lot of energy for doing things. Even after being exhausted from school activities we use to spend time on activities playing sports, cycling, and other things but nowadays we feel still tired after long hours of sleep because of the usage of devices like laptops, and smartphones to interact with social media. May be for watching Instagram Reels, Tik Tok Videos, or any web series. Even during sleeping hours, we are nowadays being impacted by the notification of social media. This notification releases dopamine in the brain and we again engage with that notification and get ourselves stuck scrolling the phone again. The effect of dopamine just works for a few minutes after that it starts affecting our health and causes a lot of health problems like itchiness and redness in the eyes, Headache, cervical problems, and many others. These are the initial stage for proceeding toward depression kind of diseases. Although we try to escape this we remain stuck in that vicious cycle.

3. Manipulation of the Mind

There is the manipulation of the mind is happening to a great extent by the big business players in the market so that their profit and sales of them can be increased. You might have seen a lot of Advertisements on social networks by different companies such companies also try to monitor your personal information so that as per your interest things can be sold to you. There are different mind manipulation activities also done by the big players so that they can change your perspective of thinking. Just because the same thing is being repeated to your eyes again and again, You start loving that thing, It's become the reason for the change to your personal opinion. In the world of the internet, It's too hard to believe in anything.

Social media is a great tool if it's being used in a great way. As there are too many demerits as well, We are being continued to use this tool in the wrong way, and because of this, we might have to face the different bad things in our life. Be aware of the things you are using on the internet, Try to spend time with nature instead of just scrolling the screen. It will help you to change your way of thinking.

CHAPTER FIFTEEN

Engineering Mindset

From our childhood, we are born with fixed dreams which might be determined by our parents, or sometimes we are inspired by people or work and we define our own dreams. You might have seen that we all had a few common dreams from our childhood like becoming a Doctor, Engineer, Scientist, astronaut, and the list is unending. Some of us get such exposure to life which helps us to reach that dreams and some are not lucky or never put sufficient effort to achieve that dreams and we end up blaming things.

If you talk about my dream, I always wanted to become an engineer just because I wanted to support my family and achieve the things which I want to achieve, After years of experience being an engineer I found that engineer is one of the super coolest domains. An engineer is enough capable to perform any kind of task that's why you might have seen it in many places engineer is always there like Banking, Medical, Army, Businesses, Finance, and many other sectors. It's all about the mindset we are being trained in. An engineer always faces pressure and challenge to achieve something.

Think Like A Engineer

"*Real engineering is not all about creating big revenues and talking fency words in meetings It's all about having attitude to solve a problem that really matters.*

- Narayan Jha"

The life of an engineer is also not easy. Engineering is not only about doing a professional degree or talking fancy words in meetings. Such kinds of things a customer care support agent can also do. A successful engineer is all about the mindset that makes him a successful engineer. A good engineer always thinks about the below-mentioned basic points that help him to create good things. It's not only about building products just because an engineer is able to think in such flexible ways he is able to successfully survive in other sectors as well.

Those are not real engineers who just work for having a package. A maximum of people are running towards the rat race of earning more with whatever engineering skills they are having. People are having professional degrees just because engineering is a trend and they can survive with a good amount of money. We never can call a person an engineer if he doesn't know the art of adding value to human life. He is just a laborer that is working for a company just to earn. Sometimes we never know whether we really add value to our job also or not. For Example: If you are a computer engineer and you got a job in a big MNC with a good package, Being an engineer you are just filling the excel sheets and creating documents is not engineering, A real engineer always thinks about creating such tools or automating them. Just because a real engineering mindset is really hard to find, This impacts the country's growth, recessions come and too many layoffs happen. The reality is we don't want to add value with a real engineering mindset, cause we are busy blaming others or the government for their things but that's, not the real way to think.

An engineering mindset is all about the attitude and the approach which is required to deal with a certain problem. They have an art of proposing solutions for any kind of problem. They never create excuses and try to find out alternatives with proper calculations. You can't learn this skill in your professional degrees. This can be learned by putting efforts into solving real problems, Facing failures, and solving them again till it's not properly resolved.

1. Things Required to perform a Task

Engineers are known for their work like if a person knows to perform things like electricity we generally call them an electrical engineer, Someone who works on the computer we call a computer or software engineer but A real engineer thinks of the resources required to perform any kind of thing. He might collect all the resources and things which is required to perform a certain task. Any kind of learnings if required he also can go through and have prepared with that.

2. Costs Required & its optimization

Everything needs a cost, There is nothing free in our life if something you are getting is free it's always going to be very expensive, Even nature follows this rule very strictly. For any kind of action or dream you always need to pay the cost behind it. The engineer always thinks about the costs associated with it in its first step. He also thinks about its optimizations which can be done so that, Things can be affordably made.

3. Experience Required for that certain task

Understand the experience which is required to complete that certain task, because if you are experienced with that thing you are aware of the issues which might come in the later phase of life. You can hire someone if you are not able to learn about that thing, This will help you to give the better chance to win a situation.

4. Managing Bandwidth & Team Work

Plan your bandwidth and team for accomplishing certain work. Bandwidth helps you to understand the availability of time, In other words, the energy for performing that work. Understand your team or create one as per the requirement. In an engineering mindset, people know the way to create a good team, Manage their bandwidth, and complete great tasks together without being overburdened.

5. Risks & Exit plans

Understand the associated risks which are involved for that certain thing. You can also go through the chapter "Risk - The Finest Teacher Of Your Life" to know more about the risk. when you know you are not going to get better results, It's a better to leave at the right time. Create an exit plan and understand when you have to leave.

6. Researches

Research is a lifetime work, This will help to understand the unknown situation. Anyone in this world can learn things by doing self-research. Make a habit to research on our own things. An engineer has the capability to research because this helps a person handle any new challenge. That's the reason an engineer mindset person is able to survive in any domain because he is always prepared for new challenges and uses research as a tool to solve a situation.

7. Outcomes of performing efforts

It doesn't matter what you are and what you want to become in your life. If you know how to think like an engineer. You don't need any professional degree from others to be that performer. You can easily become that thing with yourself because everything resides in ourselves only.

It always have a great practice for everyone - **Think Like A Engineer & Solve Real Life Problems**

CHAPTER SIXTEEN

Momentum Of Actions

Momentum is a great mechanism to increase the speed of something. We studied a lot about momentum in our school days or you might also have seen momentum on trains and plains many times but we never thought to implement the momentum in our real life. In real words, the meaning of momentum not only works on the trains or plains it also works on the mindset of performing any kind of work but we are not aware of this thing.

Momentum of actions

Momentum is the ability to keep increasing or developing the force that makes something move faster and faster. If something gets a really good momentum it becomes unstoppable. You can take the example of the train when it catches its highest speed on the track, Will it be possible to stop easily?

We can take advantage of the momentum of our actions in our day-to-day life. This is a kind of habit that we have to develop by practicing again and again. Have you ever observed when you start working on something and you are putting your actions every day, It starts going with the flow? You might have to put in very less effort once your actions come into the flow. In another word, you achieve momentum in your efforts.

Now let's think of the other scenario If you have got the momentum in your action and suddenly you stop putting your effort and you break the cycle. You took a long break for doing something else or just a break for yourself and you again start that work after getting a break. To start that work again we now have to break the resistance. We get ourselves into the cycle of comfort. This comfort works as resistance in our real life. A lot of people suffer from the pain of breaking this comfort that's why some said right:

No Pain Means No Gain

If you are capable enough to get the pain definitely you will be able to break the cycle of comfort. Once you know to work out of your comfort you will be able to generate momentum in any kind of action. You will be by default unstoppable in any case. Even the toughest kind of work will be able to complete. This momentum of action also creates consistency in your work and your intuition power for that work increases and you start working that work with your unconscious mind as well.

Any kind of work which you start and you are planning to take a break. Make a rule either don't overburden yourself every day so that you need a break or still you are planning to take a break at least put your 10% of effort into that work, In this way, you will be able to do that action every day without stopping and momentum of actions can be retained. There are a lot of people who puts their 200% effort on the first day itself and from the next day, week, or month they don't have enough energy to continue that work. Because of this energy breakdown happens in our body and momentum can't be achieved in your work.

You can be good at anything if you are capable enough to create momentum in your action in a consistent way. The momentum of actions is all about managing the internal energy in such a way that we can start putting our efforts into the long term and if you are able to do your things with a long-term mechanism you will be able to do anything and achieve every dream of your life.

A good momentum of your actions can bring a lot of things into your life. You can get the gift of good health by putting the action every day for your exercises and good quality food. Momentum is not only about doing a thing every day but also about increasing the pace with little amount so that it doesn't much impact you. You can make good relationships by spending a good amount of time with your loved ones as well. A lot might think that how the momentum of action is going to work here to improve any kind of relationship. It's actually quite simple. When you start giving time to your loved ones with great momentum you start spending true quality time with them, You start understanding good or bad things about that person and you can help them or bring something that makes another person better. In this way, any kind of thing can be achieved in our daily life with the power of using the momentum of action.

Your momentum of action works like sharping the edge of a knife, It's a continuous process, If you will try to cut something with a very sharp edge definitely it would be much easy to cut similarly the more will be momentum in your efforts, The more easily your task is going to be accomplished, It's always great to retain the momentum of your action without a single break so that all achievement can be achieved with one shot.

CHAPTER SEVENTEEN

Why & When Choose Discomfort Out Of Comfort

"Success" is an amazing word that we all want to achieve in our life. Everyone doing a huge effort to get that. We all have different meanings of success as well. Many talks about success definition and its achievement guide are being floated around over the internet. Many of them say that if you want to get things back to you you have to get yourself into the discomfort zone and put in a lot of hard work so that you can get anything that you might desire.

Comfort plays a resistive role in our everyone's life. Due to the spread of social media, we all are in the stage to get things as soon as possible with very fewer effort. Not everyone is interested to get into the discomfort zone and achieve things. This is not somehow wrong because if you are efficient enough with your brain power to get things back to you without getting yourself stuck into the discomfort zone, You already possess some sort of superpower in yourself.

GET COMFORTABLE BEING UNCOMFORTABLE

Why & When Choose Discomfort Out Of Comfort

As earlier said: "*Many of them say that if you want to get things back to you you have to get yourself into the discomfort zone and put in a lot of hard work so that you can get anything that you might desire.*" This is a simple generic statement that works for everyone who doesn't have anything or with no luck. Having clarity on whether you require to be in a discomfort zone is always necessary. There are also a bunch of people found doing unnecessary efforts just because of jealousy with some other friend cause that friend is also doing the same, We all must know not everyone has the same assets and not everyone has the same appetite, So just comparing your failures with other's success and making yourself in discomfort just because some other is doing is another level of stupidity and you are making yourself into the unnecessary discomfort.

It's not a race in which you have to come first or it's not any exam in which you have to pass. it's just a journey of life in which you have to enjoy each moment of life and experience the failures, successes According to your appetite you have to decide whether you should be uncomfortable or not. The results behind that uncomfortable zone should be always clear. Some people get comfortable being uncomfortable because in those cases they love doing things or they get adapted to the situation. Such people can live at any stage of their life.

There might be some cases where getting yourself comfortable is not an option but it's a choice, Doing exercise can bring you great benefits to your physic but not everyone is in the race to make a good body. Such things only come by choice, It actually the real commitment to yourself whether you want that thing or not, If you really want, Understand the result behind it and Know its "**WHY**", then only decide whether according to your resources or assets, you deserve to be in the uncomfortable situation or not, only then make yourself uncomfortable otherwise be in your comfort, enjoy and experience the journey of life. You are the only driver of your life to understand it better and run this vehicle in an efficient way so that very little maintenance would be required in the further stage of life and we can reach our destination with very few hiccups.

Self Realization & Improvement Habbit

You might have heard that "Your **consistency is the key of success**" but let's try modifying this quotaion from "**Your consistent mistakes are the real key of success**" because once you start the journey of learning we start with alot of mistakes, Having a courage to accept and improve that mistake is the real sign of worrior. Its not bad to do mistakes but repeating the same mistake is always bad cause life is too short for doing the same mistakes again and again. Here also comes the role of habbit. we always heard that adapt with a good habbit but at last we end up with working with bad habbits.

Habbit is something that we develop while practicing some sort of thing again and again so that our whole body gets use to it and we are able to do all those things very easily with our uncouncious mind. If you are gone with adapting your good habbits then you might get alot of great and bright things in future. Now think if you are got stucked with some bad habbits you will start getting alot of bad results. You might end up with failing all the times as well. Having alot of failures might also demotivate you. whenever something bad happens or some sort of mistake we generally express "**SORRY**" for that thing. In reality that sorry means nothing for any one or to yourself if you are not able to realtize that mistake and you are not trying to improve by not repeating that mistake again. We are using the sorry to stay away from the mistakes or to avoid the awkward situation. Instead of that we should start acting on mistakes by not repeating that.

Similary Self realization and improvement is one of the good habbits that makes us our own improved version everytime. This gives a chance to introduce yourself with new person which is better than your previous one. Its similar like upgrading a bug free software from latest one. We can use a diary to log everything whatever we are doing in our daily life. This works as a history for your efforts, successes, failure, good or bad things. We can use this logs to monitor the stuff and improving with a new solution.

A good human is only that we understand the problem find the root cause and find remedy for it. How you gonna find solution if you are not able to find our the problem. We generally forget things easily which is not important for us. This diary works as log it covers everything about yourself. This also helps you to meet the 5 years before person. You can easily judge with that whether you are on right track or not. You can modify your things as per those logs.

To get into this habbit you should be very humble and down to earth person. You should not have any relation with "**EGO**" as well because accepting your probelms, mistakes and a bad feedback needs alot of courage to accept. Once you learn to accept those you take one step ahead to improve your newest version of yourself.

Self Realization & Improvement Habbit

Those person who goes on the track of self realization and improvement habbit, They are the most honest person for their ownself by the way there is no good use to lie with yourself when even no one is watching you.

Realization about your things with time is also matters, Its kind of self restrospection to yourself. Those who don't realize their things on time, sometime they have to pay the highest penality. Its always good to adapt such good habbits on time. This makes you always prepare for the change kind of feeling. You never got stuck in one position. Realization and improvement habbit is one of the good habbits because if you got stucked in any kind of bad habbit it helps you to realize on its early stage and gives the chance to improve yourself. Its always a good practice to monitor your log diary weekly or monthly so that any kind of change in things is easily possible.

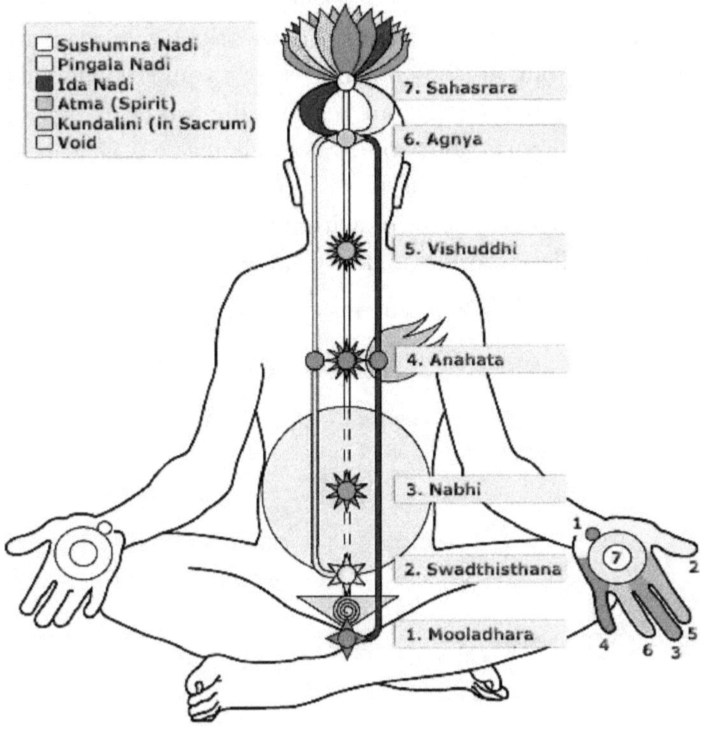

Powerful Impact of Self Realization

When you get self realized you starts the power of acceptance which is kind of real meditation with yourself and you are able to achieve the state of patience, peace and other many types of energies which is in you. The more you practice this habbit, the more powerful and improved you are going to be. Once you start completing different stages of self realization you starts controlling your senses (Indriya), Controlling your senses will give you the ability to understand good and bad things, also you will be able to control your desires as well, Just because of our desires itself we are living such stressfull life and got ourself stucked in different problems, This works for most of us throughout our life but not one tries to understand this and break so that happy and peaceful life can be achieved. The most important reason to get self realized is so that we can start giving value to love ones, nature and all the important aspects of our life without much worrying about the materialistic world which is just another trap.

CHAPTER NINETEEN

What Exactly is Financial Freedom ?

A famous talk that is happening in the current world of the internet is Financial Freedom. Everyone using their Microsoft Excel to give the feel of financial freedom and make you understand the importance of investment.

Financial Freedom

We all want to be financially free so that we can buy whatever things we want, We might go for a world tour or whatever the things required or things we think to do. We never made a pause to think about how much extinct is this really possible. Can we really get financial freedom after getting so much money in our life without getting stuck in the trap of money?

Financial Freedom

We might have seen some great financial investors like "Warren Buffett", "Rakesh Jhunjhunwala", "And Elon Musk". After getting so much net worth somehow they are also stuck in the cycle of monitoring the markets and managing their net worth things without having time for themselves and their loved ones. How many of them are going on a world tour? Warren Buffet never thought to buy big smartphones or things he can get at his early age, It is good that he knows the value of things but then what's the use of that huge net worth if it's not being used for some purpose as well, Rakesh Jhunjhunwala was not able to buy good health with that money. Elon Musk is still living in the cycle of fighting with other agencies and solving problems with their own things even having bigger net worth comes with big responsibilities and big problems as well. There is no such use of that high net worth if it's not being used for making our life easy at a right time. What's the use of having such a net worth which is not giving good health, you are not able to buy time and do those things which you might love with peace and ease.

This becomes very hard to come from this huge money trap once you get stuck in it because a lot of things depend on you at that stage and the impact will be really more if you think to quit. It just looks cool that you are an owner of such a huge net worth but we never think about the consequences behind it, Generally, our real net worth is our family, friends, good food, time, nature, and other important aspects of our life but just getting things fast and shortcut way we stuck in such traps. Now the question arises what are the real ways through which we can achieve real financial freedom without getting stuck into the trap of the money cycle?

It's very much difficult to achieve financial freedom because even if you do a lot of calculations on excel you will be financially free till there only because the economic conditions also matter a lot but we can't say it's impossible on the other hand you might have a question that then how much money is required to financially free. No one has the exact answer to this. Some people say 1 Million, and Some assume 10 Billion. This much of money even becomes zero when an economic crisis happens. Is your million, billion of money still going to help you to be financially free? I think the answer is NO.

"Sri Lanka" economic crisis is one the great examples of the same. People were paying thousands of currency just for the piece of bread. Money even becomes zero when such things happen. There are a few strategies that can be discussed which will help you to be financially free without much worrying about the future and other things. This is also gonna help you to be even rich in times of crisis as well. Let's see some common things and crucial steps which we can consider for the basics of planning your financial freedom plan.

Understand Needs & Wants

To achieve your financial freedom, Make you sure need your needs, wants and the differences between them. You should be mature enough to categorize all these in a proper manner. Add all those things bring in to the bucket of needs which are compulsory to live your life for instance food, house, electricity, and other essentials which you can never deny in any case. Now consider adding those things into the wants which you want in your life for the luxury purpose but not compulsory to required and don't have a big impact on your life. This will help you to categorize how much money you required to be financially free.

Calculate Your Yearly Expense

Now you are clear with your needs and wants, Add those needs and wants into the excel or notebook and calculate the total for both of the categories. This is gonna help you the amount which you yearly consume for your needs and wants. This is a number that we need to consider automating with some sort of assets, businesses, or something which generates money or its alternatives.

Optimization

Optimization is the real and crucial part of this whole step. Now we have finalized the needs and wants of our life. In this step, we will try to prioritize things. There might be want that could be unnecessary for that instance of time which could be easily avoided and prioritized at last so that automating these expenses could be made easy and faster financial freedom can be achieved. The cheaper is your pleasure, The less amount of effort or time required to be financially free.

Now using the steps like **Understand Needs & Wants, Calculate Your Yearly Expense, and Optimization** will help you to give insight into your financial requirement. Another step is to find out ways to automate the earning potential with some of the passive sources so that even if you are sleeping or going on vacation your urgent things should not be impacted. To make things passive at least you must require a few things like one constant income that you should already have. so that using its power we can make another passive source of income. There are also other ways to generate passive income as well for that at least you need to invent either your knowledge or time then again it becomes the active source of income but make sure something one income is necessary.

Investments:

The income you are getting you can use that income to create passive income through instruments like creating FD, RD's, Stock Market, Mutual Funds, or any other investment instrument. You should be always aware of the risks around these instruments. You can invest accordingly so that your needs and wants money can be originated from the returns of these instruments. You have to do a great deep analysis to make things possible. It could be even sometimes possible in excel or notebook but in reality, things work differently putting in some effort is always great than doing nothing because you never know which sector is going to be the best return-giving sector.

Assets:

Plan for creating assets, You can buy a car or put it for a taxi service which could be run by someone else and you can get earnings from it. You can buy land and do farming which definitely going to fulfill your needs of having food and help you to reduce yours. There are a lot of asset-creating options. Buy a house and rent it. This is your life and also have complete your choice with your knowledge and risk appetite. every asset has its own pros and cons.

Business:

Creating your own business requires a lot of experience or expertise but if you are able to develop something like a business it gives a great boost to your portfolio and you will be able to achieve your financial freedom at a very much faster rate. If you are really good at running a business you actually have better control over your own things. You can use your business as an active or passive source of income.

Finding Alternatives & Cheapest Ways:

There is always something cheap and better that exists as an alternative. Sometimes it's hard to trust a cheap thing but one always has the courage to try new alternatives. You never know which alternative is going to direct fit in. For example, if you talk about me I used cheap solar panels, solar cookers, and Natural biogas systems as the cheapest and best alternatives which automated my lifetime needs for food. The amount which I use to spend on my needs then started using in investments and creating more assets. Creating natural-based assets can help you to be protected from crisis because even if a crisis happens I will be able to create my food from my land, prepare my food from solar power and also generate my electricity from solar energy even if I have zero money I still will be able to survive without worrying about anything. In such a way, we can also increase the risk appetite and great returns or opportunities could be developed.

Debt:

To bring things early we also take debt without calculating the interest or bad consequences from it. Try to understand the game behind the debt. Stay away from debt life as much as you can. You should always use debt only in urgent cases or something you know to get profit from the debt. If you don't understand the game behind such things it's better to stay away or you want to learn and then take only that much debt so that you can manage those otherwise it might your every business, asset, or investment as well.

Plan Your Hedge:

Always be ready with your backup plan or your failure. You should create a backup for all of your investments as per the risk level so that in sudden your portfolio should not go waste. You should make your portfolio diversified in such a way that if something wrong happens in the market or position in an asset it should not impact you. For example, you can purchase commodities (Gold, Silver) as a hedge for equity. You can buy commercial properties as well this will give you a hedge when your other investments are down. You can easily get rent from it.

Make your investments in such a way that they should work in all scenarios. In all of the passive income ways, there might be different risks associated with it. The great thing is not all the sectors, domains or instruments go down at any time. You have Being financially freedom is a lifetime of work until you never have amazing luck or may have bought cryptos at 1 cent :) Just kidding.

You should have patience as well it's not a job, you should also stay away from continuously monitoring your portfolio, This makes people mentally break down. Always have a look for a weekly or monthly monitoring system if you are a long-term player.

Not everyone is having government job, Not everyone has a strong financial background and not everyone has great luck as well but we can't even stop waiting for these things to happen. The real financial free plan is something in which you can survive even with natural things and money should not be required and you are able to spend the maximum of your time with your own things. Its also an art many people from villages use this thing to live a happy and pure life. Just plan your own stuff and design the journey of your own life in your own way like a real engineer mindset so that a happy life can be made.

Proactiveness Planning & Decisioning

Proactive planning and decision are important skills in our life especially if you are planning to target some of your most important aims, This kind of mindset always gives you the ability to predict the steps which would be required to get the urgent things of future. while planning proactively we also try to find the unknowns or risks in the present scenario which can be avoided or mitigated in the upcoming future.

Proactiveness Planning & Decisioning

Once you start planning of being proactive, It helps you to take better decisions that can give you more probability to win any kind of situation. In other words, the accuracy to perform any action or taking any decision increases. All the rich people the people on a higher rank or someone who achieved something in their life use the proactive way of planning and decisions to perform any kind of action.

In earlier days, I use to spend 80% of the time performing the planning but at the time of execution, a lot of unknowns use to come which becomes the reason for my failure. Being proactive works well but only when you are aware of real facts not any kind of imaginary thing. If you are not experienced in that scenario always use the execution-driven approach to try to find an efficient solution. Being proactive generally works really better if you are already experienced with those scenarios.

In short, Those people who are proactive decision-makers are presumed to be actively engaged in a continuous process of decision-making, Hence such individuals should be able to plan their decisions in a relatively broad context, which is conducive to ensuring that they "sort out" problems and make correct decisions. If you are active in thinking or execution rather than passive in the ground of work, you are on a right track for a proactive decision-maker and planning the next track. Being willing to take action when a problem or issue presents itself is part of proactive behavior. Proactive decision-making requires that you look toward future outcomes that may result from your actions and that you are aware of helpful resources and know how to use them to help you succeed.

Let's understand this by an example, Think of a company for which we are trying to do proactive planning and according to that how decisions are made.

1. Identify the issue or problem that has to be resolved. Collect knowledge on the issue that will support your decision-making. Find out what difficulties are the real root cause, such as poor customer service or subpar products, which are causing a decline in sales, Because you are putting up the effort to pinpoint the issue that needs to be resolved, this is proactiveness. This even requires great courage.

2. Create a variety of solutions to the issue by brainstorming. If low sales are the problem, start attentively monitoring your staff to assess their customer service abilities, mentor them as necessary, or revamp some of your weaker product lines.

3. List the advantages and disadvantages of each option. One drawback is that it requires time away from your other obligations to closely watch your personnel. Helping the staff members deliver better customer service is advantageous, though, as it may boost sales and customer satisfaction. Determine how effectively the solutions will function if you apply them using the list of advantages and disadvantages.

4. To solve the issue, select one or more logical solutions. Pick the options with the biggest benefits. Put the suggestions into action and evaluate the results. Monitoring is essential so that you can adjust as per the requirement.

5. As necessary, modify the solutions or how they are put into action. Try a new strategy, for instance, if you discover that keeping an eye on your staff during

customer interactions is ineffective since they work better when observed directly. Obtain client feedback from arbitrary transactions. After the sale, get in touch with a select group of consumers by phone or email and ask them a brief series of questions to find out how they feel about the level of customer care they received.

In this way when you will get feedback from the customers, This will become the real facts and knowledge base for yourself and you can use this knowledge to tweak your logical model. This may require a lot of courage and patience depending on your needs but this will give you the best probability to win any kind of situation.

CHAPTER TWENTY-ONE

Talk To Yourself

Today is the time when we are busy with all those stuff which is urgent to us but not important. Sometimes focusing on important things can create that wealth in life that is irreplaceable with any urgent things. Let's say doing exercise is important but not urgent. Most of us focus on urgent things but not important ones. If you are doing business you might be busy managing clients, Some people are busy with their hectic schedules of doing jobs. The life of children is also not easy nowadays schools are binding every student into their busy schedule of hard work Somehow it's good to do hard work but if It impacts the physical or mental health, there is no good use in doing such efforts. We should be at least aware of what hard work is worth doing and what is not.

As we all are doing so much work, The life of people nowadays is become so stressful that we look for tons of ways to get rid of it. Many people have different solutions. Some people watch series on Netflix and Amazon Prime. Some orders food from Zomato and Swiggy, and Many are busy scrolling Instagram and Youtube reels. This shortest time of feeling stress-free becomes an addiction for multiple hours then it also starts impacting our mental and physical health. This cycle continues from the next day again until the weekend comes.

Talk To Yourself

In other words, we are jumping from one bad situation to another worst situation because of such kind of lifestyles we reduced our water intake, Exercise or any physical activities, and Meet people around us, Just because of the unhealthy lifestyles we want to live with our phones. These are the reasons a lot of diseases occurred like stones in the body, Low Blood Pressure, Headache, and many others because of which unexpected deaths are happening like heart attacks, cancer, and many more, This just started happening when we disconnected from the nature and started living stressful and unhealthy lifestyles. In earlier days such situations never use to happen. People use to live for more than a hundred years. In the last few years, the maximum life of humans is seen till 60 only. Just because we are not still thinking and continue to live an unhealthy lifestyle cause it feels enjoyable to us.

Now wait for a while, Talk to yourself when was the last time when you really spend time with nature, watching Birds, the Moon, or beautiful layers of the sun? when you spend precious time with your family and friends together, Today is the time when we just meet with relatives occasionally only, In earlier days we use to spend a lot of time with our grandparents and use to listen to their experiences of life. When was the last time when you went to the temple and spend some time chanting? We never even had proper time to think or plan for our health and finances. We just easily spend thousands on Zomatoes or Swiggies that impact our health and we never had stop and made thought about such things. Because we all are busy managing materialistic things and do not have time to talk with ourselves. Some people feel the busy culture is the coolest thing without worrying about the future consequences behind this.

We are just living for working whole weekdays and living for weekends, We should start taking action and start spending time with ourselves and made a thought what good and bad things are happening. What are the necessary actions that should be taken to make things correct that really matters to us and most importantly good for us? We should start spending time ourselves so that we can start exploring the real inside soul which is a part of supreme power. Start taking some steps to learn a few skills which also might help you to know yourself. Learn to play music, read good books, play sports, and do some creative activities whatever you like so that you can start talking to yourself. Make a diary and log everything that you do or you are trying to achieve. It works like a mirror that gives you the clarity to think beyond the things so that you can start taking actions that really matter to us.

In Geeta also said: Think with our senses, not our senses

"indriyāṇi parāny ahur indriyebhyaḥ param manaḥ
manasas tu para buddhir yo buddheḥ paratas tu saḥ
  - Bhagwat Geeta"

In the simplest word: thinking with our senses means letting our thought process be taken over by the lower desires that are usually associated with our senses. We can only achieve this stage when you will start finding our inner souls.

As a beginner you might feel really hard to start talking to yourself, If you are not doing the talk in a progressive and right way then you might also go on the wrong track. You can take the index of this book as your talk notes, You can start with any chapter and hit with small thinking actions and see what your situation is all about. For Example:

1. Plan your finances by not being trapped.

2. Managing risks and try writing your future.

3. Learn the way to use the social network with optimize way.

4. Try your way to start with meditation and chanting.

There are many more others. If you have found something and these books and ideas helped to Re-Invent Yourself. Write your story to us: info@wakeupcoders.com

Once you are gonna talk with yourself in these ways you are gonna start reinventing yourself and gonna feel happiness from inside. In reality, real happiness is just your inside-free mind once you will be skilled and knowledgeable enough with these things you start feeling enjoyable without worrying about any materialistic things, Cause you will be aware if everything is lost too, You have the capability to regenerate everything except your family, friends and whatever that is not in your hand.

Being free when you will spend time with all these, Congratulations !!! You have reinvented yourself.

Conclusion

In our life whatever kind of life you want to achieve there is nothing required other than 5 pure (Food, Shelter, Family, Pure Natural Resources, and Knowledge) elements but it doesn't mean everyone wants to live like saints because they also use these things are miles away from the materialistic things and luxurious life. It's not a bad thing to enjoy materialistic life but in the race of enjoying that life generally, we end up destroying our life without knowing the consequences.

Summary of Book

we are stuck in traps like earning more money, we destroy our health for high-return opportunities, it impacts our relationships and because of this stressful situation occurs. This is starting of bad life.

You should be either powerful enough with whatever powers like money, politics, or God-like superpowers so that whatever the thing that you want, you can get with that but that's not possible for everyone because circumstances never help, Also, if everyone will get such powers then we might end losing this whole world just because some people might be doing wrong things with that power.

It doesn't mean you can't live that happy life or you can't enjoy materialistic things or those powers. You can definitely do that if you are skilled enough. If you know the arts like understanding your brain, managing the things like risks, money, motivation, and all the arts that you might have read in this book which might help you to build a powerful impact with your efforts that can also become one of the superpowers for you. While writing this book I experienced all these skills and made impact on my life as well.

You can achieve whatever the hell you want. Generally, once again you need nothing to live a happy life instead than 5 elements and good relations with your family and friends. If you are not mature enough to understand this logic. Just be skilled enough with the arts that you have read in this whole book try making a great impact with those skills and get whatever the hell you want.

The only important thing we are required to be happy with is nothing :) because this life is one and we live only once so you should have enough time to enjoy each moment of your life with your loved ones, what's the use of becoming like **Ambani** and **Adani** if you are not able to talk, walk and live happily. In the end, everyone has to get mixed with nature only when you will die.

Create only those things which are required enough to be happy. Never be stuck in the endless cycle of creating more wealth, assets, or things for which you might get a feeling of greed. If you get stuck you should be skilled enough to understand that cycle and break it so that you can live a happy life.

You will start living a real life when you start feeling nature, having time for listening to your favorite music, doing stuff that makes you feel happy, and spending time with your loved ones so that each moment of life can be made a memory without worrying about your meetings which might happen in next hour :) or any materialistic thing of life.

Jai Shree Krishna

"No one that does good work will ever come to a terrible ending, either in the world to come."
  - Lord Krishna

Om Namo Bhagavate Vasudevaya

"When you are ignored and forgotten by the whole world. Let supreme light give a chance to guide your way and see the magic happen.
- Narayan Jha"

Important Life Lessons

Lesson 1:

An opportunity can create 1000 more opportunities, Just Hold one once for some time.

Lesson 2:

People think they are much smarter. Yeah!!! They are right, They are smart. Cause it's easy to fool someone by becoming a fool.

Lesson 3:

Your patience has a lot of potential to unlock unexpected successes.

Lesson 4:

In the darkest night of a coming storm, Always have the courage the way to fly beyond clouds.

Lesson 5:

You can't trust technology, but you can trust yourself, To make that technology believable.

Lesson 6:

Life is like a bird, There is always fear to fall down for the first time. Once you started flying you will never even try to walk.

Lesson 7:

Always Remember !! Future Means Now

Lesson 8:

You can win the whole world with single love or you can lose yourself in a war, Choice is yours.

Lesson 9:

There is always the worst situation in a particular life that never another particular can understand.

Lesson 10:

You might feel happier by purchasing expensive products. Trust me being rich is a much better feeling than just feeling rich, when your assets work itself to purchase you expensive gifts.

Lesson 11:

Being honest about everything is always a great policy because in the end there is something supreme that exists that continuously monitors and balances things.

Lesson 12:

Your simplicity is your real authenticity.

Lesson 13:

Earning The way people in urban and spending the way people in the village is another faster way to become rich.

Lesson 14:

Sometimes your big thinking capabilities work as hope in your failure times.

Lesson 15:

Starting the first day of the year with good things and wasting the rest of 364 days doing nothing doesn't make sense. In short, make your start bad that should give enough push to make rest better.

Lesson 16:

Make your effort and existence to your loved ones in such a way that you are remembered by the tearful eyes of happiness, No matter wherever you live.

Lesson 17:

Your hope fuels the action feasible enough to make your dreams come true. So never lose the spark behind hope.

Quotes Written By

- Narayan Jha

Resources

Wakeupcoders
wakeupcoders.com
Know About Us
wakeupcoders.com/about
Learn From Our Academy
academy.wakeupcoders.com
Our Services
wakeupcoders.com/services
Our Products
wakeupcoders.com/products
Social Support Initiatives.
ngo.wakeupcoders.com
Blogs And News Resources
wakeupcoders.medium.com
Partners
wakeupcoders.com/partners
Contact
wakeupcoders.com/contact

Thanks

Heartly !! Thanks For Reading My Book

I hope the experiences and lessons which are being shared in this book have helped you to reinvent yourself. If it helped let us know your story, Drop a mail @ - info@wakeupcoders.com. I look forward to hearing from you.

You will get three pages in the last section which you can utilize for creating notes for your own life. Let us know how are you planning with screenshots of those notes to reinvent yourself.

As a reference, I also shared my notes and I implemented every chapter written in this book to my life and I was able to get everything that I made dreamt of. Just have an idea and start your solo journey to execute your stuff. In case I can help you with anything just drop the mail mentioned above mail address or visit **wakeupcoders.com/contact** for more contacting ways.

My Own Re-invent Notes

Everyone talks about good things, cause talk is always easy but only execution makes sense, and it's very much difficult. There is no such use in having knowledge if you are not using it to improve your life. I got all this experience from different people, cultures, countries, and many other areas. What's the use of this knowledge and experience if I was not able to reinvent myself? Similarly, if you are reading this book just have some time to think and talk with yourself and find your way to improve your own things and achieve your dreams without impacting your happy life.

In this section, I will show you how the chapters of this book helped in my life to reinvent my own things. so this will work as my own reinvent notes. Make sure you take this as a reference and try to solve your problems with your experience and situation because everyone has a different lifestyle living in different circumstances.

when I had my first salary in Mumbai I was not having any idea about risks, investing, luxurious life, and many other things. I use to live a simple life. Even my first dream was to eat unlimited burgers at burger king in Mumbai. As covid started, the Responsibilities of home came to me and insisted me, learn all these things. With whatever money I made. I tried saving them and made them a tool.

Created natural and Artificial assets, Natural assets like solar power products that give free energy, gas, and other things for a long time, and Small farming spaces for good quality food. It saved me from extra expenses and crises as well. Created a small house and a commercial shop space for my office which can give good returns in the future. This can also be the rental income for me. Planned some of the nonpaper-based assets like investments in the USA, Indian Stocks, Crypto Currency, and FD for the safer side. In terms of emergencies created investments in life insurance and created an emergency fund of 2 years.

If we try to connect the dots in my notes all work as a backup plan for each other. Let's see how a failure occurs and how it's gonna work.

As I am having own house and commercial shop I don't have to pay any rent in any case if any crisis happens. Instead, I have 2 years of emergency fund that gives me financial freedom till 2 years to think, plan and execute further. In terms of any kind of medical emergencies insurances work as a bulletproof jacket for investments. Now if Indian or US stocks don't work well then FD is gonna create a small regular income stream. In case FD is gonna bankrupt which can only happen if the economical bad situation happens then the natural resources like food, electricity, gas and other things will naturally provide to me directly cause I am not fully dependent on the government for the same. Still, even if no money I have, I will be able to survive well, even if everything bankrupt as well.

Now definitely I was not able to create all these with one income, I learned skills that I was able to sell passively, also created liabilities to assets, and Managed the expenses in the right way. It's even not easy to create all of these in a small span of time. It might take years because for all these I had to manage the risks, motivation, planning, failures, reasons, building systems, mindset, and all those kinds of stuff which you have seen in the previous chapters. I wanted to live a free life, with all these skills I was able to create assets that work for me and get myself free from most things and I utilized my time for creating music, writing a book, and whatever I love to do. because I don't have to worry about my bread butter and the rest of the things are automated with my assets. In this way I am having control over my time and peace of mind achieved.

You can also achieve all those just plan your things in your own way. Automate them with things that you can and start living a happy life with nothing because when you will die in the end everything is going to remain here only.

So Remember: Reinvent Yourself, feel free, Live Happy with nothing.

About Author Of This Book

Hey!! Good to see you here.

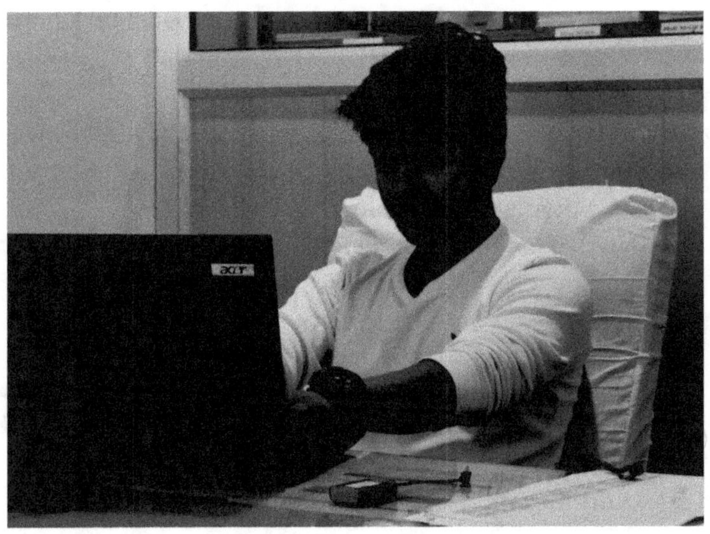

Small Talk About Me :)

I am *Narayan Jha*, Founder of **W**akeupcoders and the primary author of this book. The chapters or quotes of this book are my own self-realization which I use to feel every time when I use to get during self Introspection. Professionally I am Software Engineer and I love to do new and amazing things every day because software development is another name for "**change**" and you have to adapt it anyhow. I am an introverted kind of person and don't like much change in my things but the journey behind my software development taught me to be adaptive.

I always have a mentality to learn, teach and grow together. so I created **wakeupcoders** and in the journey of entrepreneurship, experienced great things and shared in this book. I also worked as a socially responsible person and created CodersCoders (**ngo.wakeupcoders.com**) care platform that gives support to needy people. Having experienced the journey of 70+ programming batches of students. Enjoyed teaching them and learned great things from the new generation of people as well. Created own **eCommerce** product, academy, and many services to clients for their growth of career or businesses.

Always open for any kind of open conversation. In case you have any ideas or feedback.

"*Mail us at: info@wakeupcoders.com*
Contact: wakeupcoders.com/contact"

Feel free to connect or schedule a call with me and **Let'sThink Beyond Everything Together :).**

Signing Off

- *Narayan Jha*

Notes For Yourself

Use these notes section for plan your things that will help to **"Reinvent Yourself"**

Notes For Yourself

Notes For Yourself